Anxiety to Angels

A Step-By-Step Guide to Transform Your Stress into Spiritual Connection

By

Heather Danielle

RISE INTO YOUR POWER PUBLISHING
STERLING HEIGHTS, MI

ANXIETY TO ANGELS

Copyright © 2019 Heather Danielle

All rights reserved.

First Edition 2019.

ISBN: 9781701092983

No part of this book may be reproduced in any form or by any electronic or mechanical means without permission in writing from the author, except by a reviewer, who may quote brief passages in a review.

Editing & Interior Design by Judith Kohnen

Cover Photo: Mason Harper

Contact author at heather@riseintoyourpower.com

Website:
https://www.riseintoyourpower.com/

Facebook:
https://www.facebook.com/riseintoyourpower

Rise Into Your Power Publishing
Sterling Heights, MI

Printed in the United States of America.

To Tony

Love you more!

TABLE OF CONTENTS

ACKNOWLEDGEMENTS1…………………….1
INTRODUCTION………………………………..3
CHAPTER 1 PROTECTING YOUR ENERGY……...9
CHAPTER 2 IMPORTANCE IN GROUNDING…...21
CHAPTER 3 TAKING CARE OF YOU…………….29
CHAPTER 4 EATING HAPPY……………………...43
CHAPTER 5 EMBRACING YOUR INTUITION…..51
CHAPTER 6 THE MAGIC OF MINDFULNESS…..58
CHAPTER 7 TALKING WITH YOUR ANGELS….66
CONCLUSION……………………………….79
FURTHER READING………………………..81
ABOUT THE AUTHOR………………………83

ACKNOWLEDGEMENTS

I have to start by thanking my talented editor, mentor, and best friend. Judith Kohnen, I am eternally grateful for your creative insight that you provided on the edits, interior and cover design of this book. Thank you for sharing all of your wisdom and talent with me. I am so fortunate you came into my life. Because of you, I am the spiritual teacher I am today. The next bottle of wine is on me, Bestie!

I'd also like to acknowledge my sister, Tabatha. Thank you for sharing your advice and encouragement as I wrote this book. You have always been my biggest cheerleader and your support helped me strive at becoming my best and catapulted my transformation. I cannot thank you enough for always believing in me. I love you Sissy!

To Michele, thanks for all of your help in perfecting this book and your continued encouragement. I love having you as a best friend and my go-to gal.

Thanks Mason for filling in as my assistant, for listening to my rants, and for taking the amazing photo used on the cover of this book. Your skills as a millennial are appreciated and admired. *Love you, dude.*

Thank you to my hubby bears for always lending a helpful ear and being there for me. You have always been my rock, and your continued strength never ceases to amaze me. Thank you for marrying me when I was sick and loving me back to health. *I really love you, Mocha.*

Lastly, thank you to my mom. I know you had something to do with me writing this book. You were one of my biggest fans. You've inspired me to make this the best life I've ever lived, and I know we'll be working on more books in the future together. Thanks for still being there for me, I know Heaven isn't very far away. I love you and miss you so incredibly much Mom!

INTRODUCTION

My spiritual journey began on Feb 15, 2012. It was a day I'll never forget because it was the day I started having adult onset seizures. I was only twenty eight years old and my mind and body started breaking down from the years of neglect. Doctors couldn't find what was wrong with me. The tests mostly showed up inconclusive, I was on the max dosage of some of my medications and was put on additional medication, such as Xanax, Ativan, and Prozac. I was deeply embarrassed by this but wasn't sure how to help myself get better. When no answers seemed to be on the horizon, and with my condition worsening, I finally reached out to the spiritual world.

I went to see a medium. A medium is someone who speaks to people who have passed away. At the time, I didn't know the man I made the appointment with could do this. He was an uncle to a friend, and I thought he could talk to my body and ask for answers. I was desperate. Before this, I never had a reading and wasn't really involved with the spiritual world. I had left that world more than ten years prior when I was just a teenager and I never really looked back. But here I was back in spirituality, sitting in front of a man who was communicating with my late grandmother. Honestly, it wasn't the kind of reading you seen on TV. This man spent *two hours* translating what my grandmother was saying to me. It wasn't all pretty messages either. It was clear my grandma was giving me a stern talking to. Now there's MANY people I won't listen to in my life; my loving husband is one of them-but if my Grams was going to tell me to do something, I HAD to do it. She told me more or less to *chill out*! She told me I was making things worse and I was doing many of these things to myself. Grams said who I was showing on the outside, wasn't truly who I was in the inside. She was right.

Aren't grandma's always right?

I didn't miss a beat applying the advice my grandmother gave me that day. I dove into healing videos, documentaries, and books. I took action on what the books told me to do and before I knew it, I was able to get off all of my medications. I was beyond *grateful* that I was able to get off the seizure and the anxiety pills. It wasn't an easy task. Teaching yourself to develop new *good* habits is really tough, especially if you've been living with the bad habits for many years. Not only did I have really bad habits (especially towards myself), but I was also dealing with MANY past traumas. There's a lot of things to consider on the road back to health, but not only did I get healthy, I also started embracing spiritual gifts I didn't even know I had. I went from sick to psychic!

The seven steps in this book are the most crucial steps I took to get myself to where I am now. Now, I am a psychic medium and a spiritual teacher, and I'm healthier and happier. I know the same transformation can happen for you no matter what you are looking for in life. You don't have to want to be psychic, you just have to want to be better than you are right now. Apply even one of these steps and watch change happen before your eyes.

I will use the term GUS (God, Universe & Spirit) interchangeably throughout this book. Understand that you do not have to believe in the same higher power as I do in order to perform these steps. You don't like GUS? Then, replace it with whatever term you prefer. Stay true to yourself and take what really resonates and leave what doesn't. I've been mentored and taught under many spiritual teachers and leaders, but I never really took everything they taught as gold and ran with it. (Well, maybe I did with some!) I read more, experimented, and put my own spin on most of what I was taught and then customized it to my life. I am teaching these ways to you now.

I also speak about *angels*. My take on angels will be discussed in later chapters. If you don't believe in these winged beings, I invite you to keep reading. You may learn something that will change your mind. I will give you the best steps you can take in order to have the best communication experience with them by the end of the book.

However, it isn't just angels I will be showing you how to connect to, but also guides. The topic of guides can be a book all by itself, but just know these are helpers we have on the other side most likely waiting for us to open up to their presence, so they can help make our life even better than we ever thought possible. I will also be discussing how to talk to your passed loved ones. Yes, you can do this too!

With that being said, let's dive into step number one. Honestly, this is the most important step!

Note: These steps are not a replacement for your medication nor does it constitute as medical advice. I encourage you to work with your doctor as you go through these steps. Remember, I am not a doctor, cannot diagnose, and do not give any medical advice. If you are currently on medications know that this is not a bad thing. Using medicine can help us set a good foundation so we can work on the issues that are creating the issue and what is creating the imbalance. Do not stop your medications without consulting a doctor.

CHAPTER 1
PROTECTING YOUR ENERGY

It's no secret that energy is everywhere; it can be found in and around every living thing including food, trees, and even YOU! The energy field around your body is called the aura and the energy centers within the body are referred to as chakras. The aura's job is essentially to protect the chakra centers. If the aura isn't able to do its job properly, it can affect the chakras. And well, if the chakras get affected then that affects the body!

When you think thoughts and speak words, this creates energy. The energy of our thoughts and words settle and rest in our aura. That is why it's important for you to think good thoughts and say nice words, because negative thoughts and words transform into "bad" energy and eventually can make its way into your body. What would you rather have going into your body? Happy, healthy energy, or sad, angry, unhealthy energy?

The size of your aura is completely unique. I have found the more outgoing the person is, the larger their aura. Curious, creative, and nice people seem to have larger auras compared to more quiet and introverted people. But this is just in the majority of cases. You may be quiet and introverted with a large aura, especially if you are very loving and kind-natured. A healthy, balanced aura is said to radiate about one arm's length from one's body, but can extend several feet or yards even, depending on your emotional and mental happiness at the time. So, this means that if you are sitting next to someone, or even walking close by them, you're in their energy field. This isn't always good because if that other person is thinking negative, lower vibrational thoughts, their negative stuff is blending with your aura! It creates a big issue, much like not washing your hands after you sneeze all over your fingers. You are dirtying up your aura just like you've dirtied your hands with that sneeze. Many people don't realize that what they're feeling isn't always their own feelings, but rather that of someone else whose own energies have meshed with their own.

If you are really sensitive, you may even sense their energy without it touching yours! Ever met someone and just knew what kind of person they were? It's because you tapped into their energy. Maybe you liked them and felt great being around them. Or maybe you had a bad feeling and even got sick later on that day. It's because their energy blended with yours and you got sick because you weren't protecting your aura.

Yes, you can and should protect your energy field! It is one of the most important things you can do for yourself. By protecting your energy, you will see an immediate change in how you feel. Once I started practicing protection, my anxiety diminished considerably. I truly felt like I was living in a different world—a world where I wasn't feeling overwhelmed, or on edge all of the time. If you are walking around with your energy unprotected, you are opening your aura to everyone. This can leave you feeling sick and can create illness that is caused by other people's thoughts, words, and moods. Ever get overwhelmed at a party and had to leave? This may be why. Too many energies in your auric field. You may have taken on others' emotions as if they were your own. This very well could be why you don't know why you are feeling the way you do, because the emotions were never yours to begin with.

I was at my first holistic fair when I learned about protecting my energy. It had taken me over an hour to get there, for driving on the freeway was giving me a load of anxiety. I had to take the back roads. At this time in my life, I had no idea what was going on with me. I used to be able to drive on the freeway just fine, but now I couldn't go more than one mile without feeling a wave of panic. I remember having to pull over on the side of the road with a brown paper bag, attempting to get my breathing under control and rid myself of the tunnel-vision that took hold of my eyes.

I was excited to finally make it to the fair, but then distress engulfed me the moment I walked in. I had no idea why I felt this way. Booths lines the massive space, each table with its own unique vendor with items or services to sell. People seemed to rush in and out of the lines, and I was completely devastated when I realized I couldn't handle being there. I would have to leave after all of the driving and stress. All of my excitement was wasted because I couldn't handle the anxiety caused by being in that large building. As luck would happen, I felt drawn to talk to one person before I left, and she was the one who explained everything that was going on with me without me having to say a word. She explained that I was incredibly sensitive to others' energies and was absorbing them like a mad woman. She taught me about the importance of protecting my energy, and told me the steps I needed to take. I stepped out of the building and did as she instructed me to. I couldn't believe how I felt when I returned back inside. My anxiety and panic feeling were completely gone! I walked the aisles with a smile on my face. I felt like I knew a secret no one else did. I went from feeling all sorts of emotions that weren't mine, to feeling just me. It was such an amazing experience. I felt wrapped up in my own little cocoon. I stayed for every single workshop scheduled that day, had major breakthroughs, and was still there when vendors were closing down their booths at the end of the day. It turned out to be one of the best days I've ever had.

Listed below are a few ways you can imagine protecting your energy. Your mind is very powerful and these methods will help you protect your aura and have you feeling better in a flash.

<u>Shielding</u>: Imagine a shield coming down around your body. Imagine in your mind's eye this shield coming down around you, protecting every part of you. Your shield can be any color you wish. Some healers prefer to use green because it is the color of the heart chakra and is

frequently used for healing. Others like to use white Divine Light. I personally don't have a color, thus mine is clear. Once your shield is in place, say to yourself (or aloud), "I only allow 100% love and light to come into my space and only energies for my highest good." It really is that simple. You can add your own personal touch to what you say. The main point is to tell the Universe you only accept energies of pure love to enter your space. Anything less than 100% could have a negative effect on you, and you don't want that.

Bubble: Instead of imaging a shield like above, you can imagine a bubble. I visualize myself in a bubble like in *The Wizard of Oz*. It doesn't matter what color you use, all that matters is your intention.

Divine Light: To protect yourself using Divine Light, imagine that Divine Light is washing over you, protecting you from any unwanted energies while you are taking a shower or even a bath. This is the perfect time to imagine that the water is the Divine Light washing away anything you don't need. At the same time, set an intention that Divine Light is protecting your energy for the rest of the day or night. I do this just by saying in my mind, "The Divine Light is cleansing me and will only allowing energies of my highest good to be brought into my space on this day."

Zip-Up Method: The Zip-Up method involves visualizing that there is a zipper that starts at the base of your feet and extends upward to the top of your head. With intent, you just zip yourself up. You can do with your imagination, or by physically running your fingers upwards along your body as though you are zipping it up. This one can be really fun if you have a friend present, for you can practice zipping each other up!

Cloak: Recently, I have been imagining a cloak around me that only allows energies of my highest good to come into it. I imagine myself tying up my robe and lifting the hood up and around the top of my head. I have found this to be one of the most fun ways of protecting my energy.

The most important thing for you to remember when using these methods is to set your intention. Intention is everything! If you barely imagine a bubble and mumble, "100% love and light in my space blah, blah, blah...," then your protection is likely as strong as you've just announced it to be.

I make it a habit to shield myself every day. On days I might forget, I just do it right there wherever I am standing. You can do this too. If you find yourself in a situation and you are starting to feel anxious, use one of these methods. Even if you've already done it once that day, it doesn't hurt to do it again. Sometimes others' energies are pretty strong and we need to put on a second coat so to speak.

Feel free to call upon the angels for help too. They are ALWAYS available. We'll get more into how to talk to angels, and how to hear them as well in later chapters. For now though, if your anxiety feels like it's too much to handle and your shield is weak due to your fears, call on the angels to help protect your energy. All you have to do is ask, and they will help. It's important to remember, they cannot intervene without our permission. I ask the angels for help ALL of the time, and they've never let me down.

I was walking out of a major store one day and my energy got blasted by another woman's negative energy who was entering the store. Without thinking, I yelled out loud, "Shield!" I'd sensed unwanted energy before my logical mind kicked in, and it protected me quickly from absorbing something that was not aligned with my highest good. This happened because shielding has become second nature to me. Poor woman, I could tell she had no idea what I had yelled about and it probably scared her.

Whenever anyone is talking about something that evokes emotions within themselves or within you, try one of the methods I've shared with you in this chapter. You can play around with each one to see what one works best for you. Don't worry if you don't sense or feel the imaginary shield you create around you. Trust, because it's there. By using any of these methods of protection for your aura, you can be sure that anything you *do* feel is coming from YOU. It will not strip away your sympathy or empathy for another, it will just stop you from taking on their energy and allowing their emotions to become part of your own. Making it your habit to protect your aura daily, will have you becoming a better listener. You will be less biased because you won't be feeling their "stuff."

Protecting my aura regularly has truly accelerated my path to good health. It has been a valuable tool in shifting my life around to a more balanced version. No longer do I carry the baggage of energies that once sent me reeling with panic and anxiety. It has also helped develop my psychic and mediumship abilities because I know if I am feeling anything other than my energy, then it is from the person I am reading, a spirit guide, or one of their passed loved ones.

HOMEWORK

- Go to a busy place such as a large department store, or grocery store when it is at its busiest time of day. Set your intention before you walk in to "tune-in" to others energies around you, but ask that you not pick up anyone else's energy as your own. (You can say this out loud or in your mind). Take note of how you are feeling and write down everything you experience. Ten to fifteen minutes max is all you should do for this tuning-in exercise. Leave the store and return about 10-15 minutes later. This time, set the intention to protect yourself prior to entering the place. Tune-in to the environmental energies now, noticing how different it feels. Write down the similarities and differences you noticed.

- If you are having an issue with a family member or co-worker, try shielding yourself prior to your next confrontation. Notice any difference? Remember, you can shield yourself even in the middle of a conversation. Just set your intention to release all unwanted energies from you now as you create your imaginary shield.

- If you have any difficulty or issues while driving, try any one of the shielding methods. Even though you may not be in a person's aura, you may be feeling energy exchanges between the cars, from people walking along a sidewalk, or even from an outside environment area where a lot of different kinds of energy are free flowing. This can be overwhelming to experience especially if you're very sensitive. Protecting your energy, and even your whole car can make driving a more pleasurable experience.

CHAPTER 2
IMPORTANCE IN GROUNDING

I n the previous chapter, we spoke about how energy is everywhere and in everything, including your thoughts and words. The more you think about something or talk about something, the more energy will be put into that area. It is important to establish a balance with what you are thinking about and the actions of your body. You need to have a good mind and body connection, and you can do this by grounding. Grounding is essentially honoring your physical self by strengthening your connection to this earthly plane. It is one of the most important things you can do to get balanced and to strengthen the mind and body connection.

Remember, you are a spiritual being having a human experience, not a human experiencing something spiritual. If you are really interested in matters of the mind, but are neglecting your physical body, you can become unbalanced. You may have heard that energy flows where your attention goes. This is so true! Too much energy in one area will disrupt the balance.

Of course, there are many factors that can affect the energy balance within the body, but for now, I will give you the skinny on a few things that can make you feel ungrounded and out of balance. Beware of doing the following for very long periods of time and not taking breaks for some type of physical activity in between:

- Excessive daydreaming
- Engaging in creative tasks
- Watching/reading Sci- Fi and Fantasy
- Listening to music

- Reading books like this one!

The above are completely okay for you to engage in, they may bring out the best parts of you! The thing is, you have to have a balance. If you notice, most of the above activities require you to engage your mind. If you do something that exercises those thinking skills, you should do something to also work your body to bring yourself back into alignment. You can also make sure you ground before or after engaging in these activities. Sometimes, these activities use so much of your mind and imagination that it will help bring you back into alignment by also honoring your physical self.

I remember after I embraced my abilities, I started doing fairs and psychic parties. This is where I do readings back-to-back. They are fun, but it requires me to connect so much with the spiritual realm that if I don't ground myself after every couple of readings, I find myself not even connecting to the words I am saying. I become so spaced-out that I feel like I am talking gibberish and making no sense. It is a feeling of being drunk, but without alcohol. Once I had spent hours doing readings for a party and became so ungrounded, I had to stop in the middle of the reading and ground myself. Once I did my grounding exercise, my mental clarity returned, and I was able to continue on with a fabulous reading for my client. This was one of my worse ungrounding experiences. I felt completely disconnected from my body. It felt like an out-of-body experience, and not in a good way. Many of us may feel the consequences of being ungrounded throughout our day and we don't even realize it. We become so involved in using our mind, we neglect our bodies. Even the thought of thinking about your body is requiring more of your mind than of your body!

There are a few ways you can ground yourself. Depending on where you are and how much time you have, one may work better than the other. Play around with these as well to see which works best for you!

<u>Walk barefoot on Mother Nature</u>: This is a great way to ground fast, and it's really simple. Walk on grass, the dirt, anything that is alive in nature. It will connect you directly back to the earth, nature, and yourself.

<u>Become a tree</u>: Sometimes I do the yoga 'tree' pose. Other times, I just imagine I am a tree and my toes are roots, extending down deep into the earth. (Your mind is so powerful that just the act of imagining can reap real benefits).

<u>Drink water</u>: Water comes from the earth and you are putting part of the earth into your body.

<u>Eat grounding foods</u>: Eat foods that come from the earth, especially foods that are grown under the soil, such as turnips and onions. We will go more into foods in the *Eat Happy* section of this book.

Carry stones and crystals: There are many different stones that can help keep you balanced. I have found hematite to be the most grounding stone for me, but I have found each person is different. So, play around with a stone that really resonates with you. Some options are black tourmaline, red jasper, and smoky quartz.

Pay attention to your earthly life: The more you pay attention to your physical existence, the more you will become grounded. This means paying attention to your body, finances, home, or anything of the physical world.

Spend time in nature: Maybe you can't go out barefoot, and that is perfectly okay. Just connecting with nature by spending time outside will help you ground and get you back to feeling centered. This includes gardening and physical activities outside like walking, hiking, and kayaking.

Read books: But not books on self-help, spirituality, and the like. Read books about things that happen on this earth like business, animals, and nature. Try to get your logical side balanced with your imagination.

Cleaning your house: The act of cleaning uses your lower chakras. World renowned Psychic Medium John Holland states that after readings, he will clean his bathroom. He claims that nothing can ground you more than cleaning a toilet. Try that out today.

After a day of readings, I will come home and watch action movies with my husband. I usually only watch comedies and uplifting movies, but after using my mind so much (especially with spiritual matters), I need to come back down to Earth. I find nothing grounds me faster than action and car chases!

Grounding has helped decrease my anxiety immensely. It has helped me stay in-tune with my body so I don't feel as anxious. It has helped my intuition greatly because I am more balanced, centered and aligned. I don't forget things as much when I am grounded, and I am able to focus more clearly.

HOMEWORK

- Practice at least one of these grounding methods described in this chapter. Take notes of how you were feeling before grounding, and then compare them to how you feel after the grounding experience.
- Use the following suggestions to help you "be a tree." I find these are best to do in the AM, but you can do them any time you want.
  - Stand with legs shoulder-width apart.
  - Imagine your toes are roots going down into the earth.
  - Breathe, imagining your breath going from your toes up through your body
  - Raise your arms above your head and imagine your arms are tree branches.
  - Do this for a few moments, then give thanks and start your day.

CHAPTER 3
TAKING CARE OF YOU

I cannot stress enough about the importance of honoring your human body. The mind-body connection is truly everything. When you take care of you, not only will your intuition improve, but you'll experience more peace in your life, be healthier, and less prone to ailments and disease too. Taking care of yourself is crucial when speaking with the spiritual realm because the healthier you are the clearer vessel you are for spirit. This will help you hear guidance better, and will allow for stronger communication because your body will be in the best shape to get the information.

It can be hard for many of us to take care of ourselves. We become so involved in taking care of others, we neglect ourselves. Chances are, you have heard how important it is to take care of yourself, but it's difficult to put a good self-care routine into action. Here, I will not be going over the various aspects of self-care that you have already heard of. Nor will I be going into how you should get massages often and have a spa day once in a while. (Even though you really should pamper yourself like this as often as you can). What I am covering, though, are a few basic things that can help you take care of yourself so that you can become healthier mentally and emotionally, which in turn will affect your physical state as well. The simple things I'm about to share with you require almost no time and effort, and best of all, no money!

It took me years to realize how I was neglecting my body. Of course, I took showers, brushed my teeth, and exercised intermittently, but I didn't realize I was unconsciously harming my body by neglecting it. I wasn't giving it the time and care it deserved. I have heard so many people talk smack about their body, especially their flaws. Talking crap about your body only hurts yourself and makes your self-image worse. I find it ironic when people talk about how ugly their feet are. Your poor feet, look at all of the work they do! It's time to start honoring your body and all of its hard work it does for you. Instead of looking at all of the issues with your body, try to see the good things it does for you. If you have a really poor self-image, this may be hard. Dry brushing can help. Dry brushing is where you use a body brush and you brush your skin before getting into the shower. This allows for you to assist your body in getting rid of dead skin cells, and also improves circulation along with many other benefits. They also say it can help decrease cellulite too! (Bonus!) Most importantly though, it allows for you to connect to your body! If you want more out of dry brushing, tell your body that you love it while doing it. I know it may sound silly, but it will help your body and mind get back on the same page. Instead of rejecting your body, you will be accepting it. This will help immensely if you are wanting to change anything with your body because the more you accept it, the easier it will be to change. It will create a mind/body partnership, and you will be working with your body instead of against it.

Another aspect of self-care many people have a difficult time with is breathing! Breathing is life and it is said that it is through breath that we connect. If we can breathe better, this will allow us to connect to our angels much easier. So often we are holding our breath and don't realize it, or we breathe too shallow. If you work at a computer, or are often on your computer, the odds are higher that you hold your breath and not realize it. They say the computer screen flashes faster than our eyes can catch and ignites the fight or flight response within our psyche causing us to stress out, clench our jaw, and even subconsciously hold our breath.

Shallow breathing inhibits our oxygen flow and doesn't allow the diaphragm to work like it's meant to work for us. The oxygen isn't able to get everywhere it needs to go. Just the simple act of breathing can really help your mind and body feel so much better. Have you ever seen a person having a panic or anxiety attack grab a brown paper bag like I mentioned I had to do while driving? The paper bag helps us get our breathing under control and assists our body in regaining balance. It brings us back into the present moment which is SUPER important if you have stress or anxiety issues.

Believe it or not, the odds of you breathing the wrong way is pretty high. And yes, breathing wrong is actually a thing. When you breathe in oxygen, your stomach is supposed to expand outward, filling your lungs with air. When you exhale, the stomach contracts inward. Try practicing now by inhaling, causing your stomach to swell larger, then exhaling to deflate it. Pay attention to your shoulders. Do they rise up when you breathe? If they go up, note that you need to breathe more "out" of your stomach and use less of your shoulders to breathe. This will help release tension and stress in your shoulder and neck area. Yes, the discomfort you have in those areas could be because you are putting unneeded stress on them by breathing the wrong way. Breathing the correct way will reduce stress in the body, allow you to breathe deeper and will have you more connected with your body and with Spirit.

Breathing can also really help you if you're in a pinch and having an anxiety attack. Breathe in through your nose, hold for 10 seconds, and then exhale back out through your nose. Focusing on your breath will allow you to come back to the present moment, and will decrease your anxiety because you won't be focused on what is causing the attack. Most often times, anxiety attacks happen when you are worried about a negative outcome in the future. Concentrating on your breathing allows you just for those few moments, to be in the present, and not worry about the future so you can realign and feel better.

You have some good tools in your self-care tool box now including energy protection and grounding tools discussed in the previous chapters.

You need to continue to practice with these tools because of... *energy vampires!*

Ever heard of them? They're not the blood-sucking monsters you have read about, or the pretty sparkling ones on television. They are the people who are in your life right now stealing your energy like a thief in the night. They are the people who call and vent to you on the phone, complaining about their day and how things are just horrible for them. You listen politely, and before you know it, the call ends with them feeling better, but you are not feeling so well. You feel tired, drained even. That's because you have been unknowingly attacked by an energy vampire!

What happened was an energy exchange. They released their lower vibrational energy onto you and took your good vibrational energy. Most of them don't mean to do this, it's usually unintentional.

Do not fear. You can protect yourself with the shield we discussed in chapter one, or some other protection method. Yes, you can do this even over the phone, so be sure to perform this important step. Often times we don't want to protect ourselves from our family and friends who us, but I need assure you, putting a shield up won't stop you from helping them. What it does is allow the energy they are pushing toward you to bounce off your shield. You can imagine that the energy is being transformed into loving light and released to the Universe if you like.

Do you know of any energy vampires in your life? Anyone who is calling or texting about their problems? I bet you do! Just be mindful and protect yourself when you get to chatting with them. They are not "bad" people for doing this. In fact, if they knew what they were doing, I'm sure they would feel guilty for putting the yucky energy onto you. It is human nature to vent, and to reach out for support when you need it. You just have to take care of yourself, that's all. And in doing so, you will become a better listener and can offer more sound advice since you aren't wrapped up in their emotions involving whatever is bothering them.

You can also take care of yourself by not giving too much of yourself away to others. Of course, we all want to help our family and friends but we have to be careful of doing too much for them. And yes, it is possible! Too much intervening can interfere with life lessons they were sent here to overcome.

Chances are, if you're reading this, YOU are an Earth Angel –a sensitive being reincarnated to share love in the world. Earth angels come in all sorts of shapes and sizes and feel a deep desire to help others. Many have chosen careers, such as nurses, counselors, teachers, therapists, book editors, and even tattoo artists!

Earth angels love to help others in their own unique ways. Their goal is just to leave the earth with more love than there was before they came here. Earth isn't perfect though. It is full of the unknown with lessons to learn that create a lot of challenges for us. So, we Earth Angels are often left with a bruised heart because we're more sensitive than others. We want to help, but we have to remember that each of us have reincarnated here for our own personal reasons.

We have to respect that everyone is on his or her own unique path. We can't always help or get people to see the way we see things. Our job is to merely be available when needed (with energy protection in place, mind you). To keep doing too much for them is teaching them not to be responsible for themselves and keeps them from making their own choices in life. It is up to the Universe to intervene in paths in which intervention is needed. It isn't our call to step in with our own opinions and courses of actions all of the time. If you have tried to help someone two or three times, then step aside and allow the Universe to come in and work its magic. You will know when it's time to step in again; the Universe will let you know.

Honestly, it is wrong of us to deprive someone of their rock bottom. I know at first reading that sentence may seem shocking, but isn't it the truth? Have you ever hit rock bottom or know someone who has? Have you witnessed firsthand how they transformed because of these situations? Rock bottoms are opportunities to learn, to trust, and to transform! I am so grateful that no one deprived me of my rock bottom. In fact, I had many of them, and I bounced off of them several times before realizing something had to change. I look back on some of my rock bottom moments, and I am grateful for them. Being homeless as a single mom while going to college was one of the toughest things that ever happened to me. Not only was I struggling to find my son and me a good home, but I was struggling to keep my high GPA while working full time. This time brought my son and me closer, and it really required me to rely on a higher power because I honestly had no other choice. I kept my faith and with divinely guided help, I was able to find us a home just in time for the holidays. I was also able to graduate with high honors!

Humans in general though, don't like change. We're creatures of habit, and sometimes we have to be forced out of our comfort zone to make the necessary changes in order to benefit our lives. You grow and learn more when there is friction. I like to think I could've learned just as much if I wasn't given the horrible situation of being a homeless single mom, but when I really think about it- nothing could've created those learning opportunities like this one did. It strengthened my bond with Spirit and I was able to show my son what hard work and perseverance could do. He knows now that even if you hit rock bottom, you can always climb back on top. I am grateful I had this experience, it showed me how strong I was and what I was truly capable of.

Can you think back at a time in your life when you had hit rock bottom or something close to it? Even though it was so tough at the time, can look back and see how it helped you see things differently? Even though it may have been so tough at the time, can you look back and see how it helped you see things differently? Maybe because of it happening, you were able to make better choices, and those decisions helped you out of your own rut? I invite you to allow this to happen to others in your life as well. So often we're eager to jump in to help other people. Many of the times it is because we don't want them to go through what we went through, but don't they deserve to write their own transformational story?

Letting go of the guilt for not helping others can be tough. It really comes down to one key ingredient ... *trust*. You have to trust. Whenever I find it difficult to see the bigger picture being painted, I look outside. I look at the clouds, the stars, the trees, and all of the colors of the world that I often take for granted. This brings me back to the beauty and the amazement of the miraculous world we are living in. We may not know all of the whats and whys and how comes, but there is something more going on in and around us that we can't comprehend. It is something powerful, amazing, and well, something smarter than all of us.

Think of your life as a movie. We are all the producers and stars of our own life. The people in our lives are our co-stars. Since we are the producers, we get to choose who stays in our lives and what parts they will play. There will be good times in our movie, bad times, and times that are just plain crazy. Isn't that what makes a good movie "good" though? The unexpected events and plot twists can create adventure in a movie. Sometimes the scenes in a movie are needed in order for the cast to grow, learn, and create their happily ever after.

Firing a cast member (aka a friend or family member) from your life can be a tough pill to swallow but sometimes it is needed. I have learned though, that it doesn't always have to be permanent. Sometimes, we just need a break from a person. This doesn't have to be a boyfriend or girlfriend either. It can be a toxic parent, an annoying friend, or a grumpy neighbor.

If there is a person whom you have shielded yourself from and tried every trick in the book to help make the relationship between the two of you better, it may be a sign that you need a break. You don't have to make a declaration that you are taking a break from this person on social media, or in a long heart felt letter to send to them. You just have to set the intention this is what you want. Let Spirit know and allow the process to unfold naturally and it will if that is for your highest good at the moment. You just may notice the person gets really busy, or can't get into their social media account. It can be simple things that Spirit puts in the way to allow this break to happen.

Even though these tips have really focused around other people, it really helps you create healthier boundaries so you can feel better. The more energy you give to yourself, the better you will be in all areas of your life, because you will have more energy to use as patience, as understanding, and most of all, love. If we keep draining ourselves caring for others, we will be too tired and weak to be any use to them.

Taking care of you will help you feel better about you and will help you connect to yourself. Much of my anxiety stemmed from the fact that I had completely lost myself in what others thought I should be, what I should wear, talk like, look like, etc. Taking care of me helped me live each day better. I noticed people leave my life who weren't in it for my highest good, and then after a break from them, they came back into my life with much better energy. The Universe noticed this vibrational change and put more people in my life that matched my new energy. You keep things in your life when they are a vibrational match. The discord comes when these vibrations are mismatched. This is why eliminating them from your life, or taking a break from them is helpful. You can get back into balance. Once you tell the Universe what you want, and what you will and won't put up with in your life, it will oblige. The Universe will start bringing people into your life who are a vibrational match with you, and then you'll start manifesting people in your life that lift you up and make you happy instead of wearing you out.

You HAVE to take care of the most important person in your life, which is YOU! Without you in your life, you wouldn't *have* a life. I know that may sound silly, but you need to hear it. YOU are the most important person in YOUR life, because there wouldn't be a you without YOU!

HOMEWORK

- Imagine your life is like a movie playing on a large screen. You are the star and the director. You have a backstory and your family and friends are your co-stars.

- ✓ Take a moment and think about what kind of movie your life looks like right now. Is it a romantic comedy? A thriller? Are there too many characters?

- ✓ Now think of what you would want your movie to look like? An adventure? Or like a mellow sitcom?

- ✓ Do you need to recast any characters? Do any supporting characters need a bigger role?

- Practice shielding and not shielding your energy while your friend is on the phone venting to you. See if you can notice the difference in the way you feel when you are shielded versus not shielded.

- Throughout your day, take note of how you are breathing. Do your shoulders rise up when you breathe in, causing more stress upon them? Try as often as you can to breathe deeper and better.

CHAPTER 4
EATING HAPPY

I hope you like the title of this chapter, Eating HAPPY. It's not necessarily about eating healthy, even though I TOTALLY recommend that! The truth is, what is healthy for one person may not be healthy for another. We've all seen people who eat horribly and live great lives, and you've probably seen the opposite—a person who eats very well but is always sick, or something is always physically happening with them. There may be more than one factor affecting these situations. One thing that *is* the same is that each of these situations is proof that our bodies are uniquely different. What works for one may not work for the other. We cannot take a one size fits all approach to eating.

Changing my eating habits changed my life when I started to have seizures. The lack of self-care over several years had suddenly crept up on me. If you've ever been stressed out, worked multiple jobs, or dealt with a lot of family & friend issues, you know what I am talking about. You start neglecting yourself by eating inadequately or you stop exercising and doing those things that are good for your body.

When our body isn't working properly because we are eating things that we're allergic to, or that which is not good for us, it affects our mind's ability to think clearly and perform like it should. I know coffee causes me to feel jittery and makes me feel like I have extra energy in my lower arms. This may sound odd, but it's how it affects me. If I didn't know this was coffee doing this to me, I could experience more anxiety because I wouldn't know what was causing me to feel that way.

Some people may be more sensitive to food ingredients than others, and just because it is something healthy doesn't mean it's good for YOU. Meat and animal products are a great example. Yes, they are an excellent source of vitamins and protein, and some people can eat them without any issues. Others, like myself, cannot for a variety of reasons. Some of us are even sensitive to the energy from the animal we've eaten.

I NEVER thought I'd believe it, but it's true. When we eat animal products, we also consume the leftover energy of the animal. If you think about it, energy is everywhere and in everything, right? That includes animals. So, when we eat their bodies, isn't it safe to say you are also consuming the energy of that animal? Of course, their soul is gone, but there's still energy inside of that body. When you consume meat, you may be taking on some of the animal's energy. This can cause you to feel energies connected to the animal, which could increase your anxiety, stress, and more. I recommend you say a blessing over the meal you are about to eat and ask Spirit to take away anything that isn't for your highest good. This is a smart thing to do even if you don't think you are sensitive to any energies you are about to consume. Sometimes, this can affect us subconsciously. If you are going to consume animal products, I always like to add a thank you to the animal for allowing its body to give mine nutrients. It is really important to know what foods you are sensitive to, and those that you are completely fine with.

Try the elimination diet by removing certain foods from your diet, and then re-introduce them later to see if you get a negative reaction. This has helped me greatly, but doing it with consistent body scans is most beneficial. Body scans are when you scan your body and tune into it paying attention how you are feeling at the moment. You take note of any tension, stress, sensations your body is feeling. When you do this before you eat and then after, it will help you see how your body is reacting to the food you consumed. Some foods can create all sorts of different effects on the body that you may not be aware of. This method will help you to see if the food you're ingesting is causing the issue, or if it is something else causing your symptom. Each time you add a new food on your elimination diet, do a body scan periodically throughout the day, because sometimes it may not manifest into an issue for hours or even days later.

Even though I was able to get off my seizure medications, it didn't stop my declining battle with health. My body had been pushed to the limit, and I underwent many tests and surgeries to help my body correct itself. Everything I have learned that worked for me centered around eating foods that were better for me, not necessarily the foods that are deemed 'healthy' for everyone.

A perfect example was in 2016 when I was diagnosed with Crohn's disease. I had ended up in the hospital with an NG (nasogastric) tube not able to drink, eat, or have any ice chips for days! I wanted to die to be honest. The doctor informed me of how serious the situation was and informed me that if my body didn't heal itself soon, I would have to have emergency surgery for a colostomy bag that I would have to wear as an attachment to my abdomen for the rest of my life. Luckily, my body did heal the issue so I avoided the surgery. Afterwards, so that I would never go through that ordeal again, I looked seriously at some alternative options-a vegetarian diet, a dairy-free diet, and then a vegan diet. Unfortunately, none of them really helped. Then, during a meditation one day, I did a body scan and heard my body crying from what I was eating. It was during this meditation, I was able to connect the dots between my Crohn's and gluten! I had been tested for celiac disease – an autoimmune disorder where the small intestine gets damaged when one eats gluten. Only tests showed that I did not have the allergy. I eliminated gluten just to see what would happen, and sure enough- my stomach spasms ceased! To this day, by listening to my body I can tell whether the food I eat contains gluten or not. I am excited that I was finally able to find the source of my stomach spasms and what was worsening my Crohn's symptoms.

Am I telling you that you should become a gluten-free vegan in order to be healthy? No, nothing is further than the truth! You may be a person who thrives off of animal products, and whose body doesn't have the issue with gluten. You will just know your body better by doing these body scans and choose foods that makes your body thrive. You may be really surprised like I was by what food is causing your distress and how it is manifesting in your body.

Changing your diet to fit what is best for you can really make a difference in how your physical body functions, and how it affects your emotional body as well. This isn't just about getting off of medications, but it is about getting some more answers as to why your body is feeling the way it is. So far, if you protect your energy, ground yourself, and take care of your human body along with watching how foods affect you, then you are well on your way to transforming into a completely healthy new you!

When you take care of you by eating better and moving more, you become a clearer vessel for Spirit. Have I said this already? Sure have, because it's true! When you are a clearer vessel for Spirit, you're are able to get clear messages with more details.

HOMEWORK

- Perform a body scan on yourself by asking all energies that are not yours to step outside of your space (just in case you've picked up unwanted energies from others).

- Bring your focus to the top of your head and follow it down your entire body, paying close attention to how you are feeling. Do you have tension in your arm? Maybe you feel anxious? Whatever it is, take note.

- Drink or eat whatever may be questionable in your regular diet (less ingredients within the food item is best so you can better pinpoint a specific thing that doesn't agree with you). Wait 15 minutes and do another body scan. Has anything changed? If not, try doing another scan later on, possibly in an hour, 4 hours, or the next day, and see if you notice anything different.

CHAPTER 5
EMBRACING YOUR INTUITION

Yay! We have finally made it to the subject of intuition. This is one topic that I am very passionate about. I am hoping this chapter will be life-changing for you, because it can be if you just open up and allow it.

You may have noticed that you have different voices in your head. Don't worry, it's completely normal. You're not crazy. I narrow the voices down to two inside my own—my ego voice and my intuitive voice. Picture the angels on either shoulder. The good angel is your intuition, and the mischievous one is your ego.

The teaching craze these days has been about the acronym EGO—*Edging God Out*. I used to believe this, but realized that this isn't really true. The ego isn't a bad guy, it's just gotten a bad rep. It is part of your mind that analyzes your reality and was created to protect you. This worked well back in the caveman days when we needed it for survival. We still need our ego, just not as much. Often times, the ego is left to go wild, with no boundaries or rules, much like a toddler would be without supervision. Because of this, it is often the louder voice in our minds.

The voice of intuition is very different. It is often seen as your Higher Self talking to you or your gut instinct. It is what gives you the feeling in your belly when you think something is not quite right. It really is your best friend. You were born with this intuition, but sometimes we are taught not to listen to it. Our parents and other family members have had good intentions, but they may unknowingly push our intuition down by telling us we're wrong and they're right. They may be doing this out of your best interest, and think they're protecting and helping you. If this keeps happening, though, it teaches us not to listen to ourselves.

This may discourage this voice, and it becomes harder to hear after time. Soon it becomes barely a whisper. When we are constantly not listening to ourselves and just listening to others, this pushes a part of ourselves away, and this can create more anxiety, stress, and worry for us. It truly creates turmoil within our body and our mind, for we are actually rejecting ourselves. We cannot live in harmony if we are creating an inner war against ourselves.

When you are taught to listen to another's voice more so than your own you become unbalanced. This can cause the ego voice in your head to get louder and your intuition voice gets pushed down and away. It doesn't have to be that way. The more you can listen to your intuitive mind, the louder it will become for you.

Embracing your intuition can be a little tough. Especially if you have spent years pushing it away. If you have learned to not trust yourself, gaining trust sometimes can be a little difficult. It is possible though to get it all back. Once you do, your entire life will change. You will get to know yourself again and become your own best friend. You'll find that you will make better decisions, have less self-doubt, and the war you are fighting against yourself will cease. You will feel more confident, more aligned, and you'll finally understand yourself better.

Once you start aligning with your intuitive mind, your thoughts will come as never before. You'll notice a difference that can truly change in your life in wonderful ways. Think of a time when you felt like you should do something, yet for some reason, you didn't listen. Then later, you realized that thought was correct and you could've kicked yourself in the butt for not listening to your first inclination. It's the one that may have told you that you left the coffee pot on, but you didn't think you did until you came home to see that sure enough, the voice was right; the coffee pot was indeed on. THAT is the voice I am talking about!

The Voice of your intuition is abundance based. It doesn't judge, give reasons, nor is it ever mean. It's the innocent part of yourself and it doesn't cry for attention. That is probably why it is difficult for some of us to hear. The ego on the other hand, is bossy, always giving reasons why you should or shouldn't do something. It argues with you, and creates drama in your mind.

It's like you have two toddlers in your head. One is wild and crazy, gets all of the attention, and the other toddler is quiet and feels like it isn't loved because the other toddler gets everything it wants. You just need to create balance here, give your intuition some attention, and when you hear it, take the action it suggests. The more you listen to it, the stronger it will get.

If you're wondering what to do with the *ego toddler*, just remember children love boundaries! They just don't know they do. So, create rules, talk back to it, but don't go down the negative rabbit hole it's trying to lead you down. Listen to it, thank it, and give a short answer it if needed. Talking with the ego is much like fighting with a toddler, you can't win against its logic. So, only acknowledge what it is saying, give thanks, and carry on. Give this voice an accent, or give it a name. My ego's name is Princess PITA. (PITA=Pain in the Ass). This can help you take it less serious, which is important if it is stressing you out. Doing small steps like this will help the ego voice soften and allow more attention for the intuitive toddler to have their say. This establishes balance and will help you know which voice is working for your highest good.

I can promise you, if you start using your intuition, you will be saving yourself a lot of time and heartache. I find listening to it a lot of fun, and this is the very first step to hearing your angels! Doesn't it make sense that you would first have to hear yourself before hearing the spiritual realm? You have to decipher whether it is you talking, or someone else. Your anxiety symptoms should decrease as well, because you will have more self-trust and self-awareness. It truly will accelerate your ability to talk with your angels because you will be able to tell when it's them talking to you because you will already be familiar with the voices in your mind.

HOMEWORK

I know you're excited to try out your intuition! Well, there are MANY things you can do to strengthen your intuition. Here are some things to help you tap in:

- Listen to the voices in your head for one full day and try to decipher which is your ego and which is your intuitive higher self. Is one voice much higher in tone than the other, or do they seem pretty balanced?

- When you are at a restaurant, coffee joint, or the like, and you're either working there as a server or just sitting at a table look around you and see if you can pick up on what a person will order before they do. You can start off by seeing if it will be a hot or cold drink. Then, ask yourself what kind of food they will order. I used to do this when I was a server. When I approached a new table, I would suggest a drink I thought they may drink. It was a fun game. You can do this with friends when they come over and it will really help strengthen your intuitive voice.

- Play heads or tails with a coin. Or get out a deck of playing cards and guess what card you will pull. Using your gut instinct try to choose whether it will be a red suit or a black one? Try to intuitively pick the number, the type of suit, whether it's a face card or not.

- Guess what elevator door will open first when you approach more than one. Also try to intuitively pick up what floors the elevator will be stopping at before any buttons are pushed.

CHAPTER 6
THE MAGIC OF MINDFULNESS

I really wanted to name this chapter, Magic of Meditation because to truly connect with yourself and the spiritual realm, meditation is THE KEY ingredient. You can try to get passed it but you won't get too far because Spirit communicates through thought. We will go over other ways they communicate, but their first language so to speak, is thought.

I know how difficult meditating can be, especially if you are suffering from mental distress. Personally, my worries and anxieties were so high, I didn't trust my surroundings enough to close my eyes. I was just too scared to meditate by myself. In fact, I found a local monastery and started meditating with Buddhist monks. Being in the peaceful environment with them allowed me to put my guard down, close my eyes, and have great first meditation experiences. However, there is something else you can do to help calm your mind so you can notice and hear Spirit, and that is through *mindfulness.*

Mindfulness is about being in the present moment with no judgement, fears, or any analyzing of the past or future. It is all about putting your attention to what your five senses are picking up in the moment.

Have you ever driven somewhere and realized that you have no memory of how you got there? Or have you ever found a bruise on your body and have no recollection of what might have caused it? You were probably on autopilot.

Autopilot is when your body and mind know a task so well that things get done without you being conscious of it. We do this all of the time when walking, eating, driving, and even working. This can be a very useful tool. Thank goodness we don't have to tell our mind to put our left foot forward, and then our right foot forward when we walk. Luckily, that memory is stored inside us, and thanks to our built-in autopilot, we can do many things without thinking.

The issue is, though, we lose too much awareness of what's actually going on in our life. We learn to multi-task while on autopilot and get lost in our thoughts about yesterday, tomorrow, and everything in between. We don't realize that we're living for every moment except the most important one—the *present* one! Then we become unbalanced, for we are living on too much autopilot. I am guilty being on autopilot a lot. It's just because I love daydreaming; I love being creative and deep inside my mind. I had to learn to come back to the moment and learn how to turn autopilot off, because I found myself so secluded inside my mind, I was missing out on my life!

One really big way people can abuse autopilot is while eating. I remember back when I ate not-so-healthy and grabbed two hot dogs for dinner. When I sat down in front of the couch to eat them a minute later, they were gone! I couldn't find them anywhere. Not on the floor, not in the trash. I didn't have a dog, and my son wasn't home. The hot dogs were nowhere to be found. I know now that I aimlessly ate them on autopilot without even thinking. The sadder part of this story is that I still felt hungry and had to go get more food! Has that ever happened to you?

Mindfulness is the exact opposite of this. It says to the body, "Thanks for the autopilot option, but I am going to be an active participate in this moment." Whenever you feel autopilot taking over, you can get back in the driver's seat. The more you practice, the easier it will become. It is a workout for the mind much like meditation is. It's like bringing your mind to the gym. The more you exercise in doing this, the better your results will be.

Being mindful of what you are thinking about is essential for connection. Since Spirit communicates through thought, you will have to catch what they say when the thought comes in. Sometimes they talk to you out of nowhere when you least expect it, and sometimes it comes into your mind so fast, it is hard to catch what they say. So, the more you are in the moment, the easier it will be for you to communicate with them. Paying attention and being in the present moment is really how psychics and mediums get their information. They pay attention to thoughts, feelings, and sensations that weren't there before they decided to connect with their client. If mediums have a crazy, busy mind and they are not in the present moment, the information coming through for them from Spirit may come through jumbled and unclear.

You can really miss out if you're not in the moment. Not only will life pass you by more quickly, you will have less memories of what you are doing on a daily basis. A busy mind may cause you to be more stressed out and worried about things that haven't happened yet.

I remember prepping for my first mediumship gallery reading. I was going to have just a few people over at my house to practice as my audience. Before they arrived, I was blessing my living room for protection, and clearing out any negative energy. I did this to raise the vibration of the room and to set the intention for the night. When I walked around the room, I stayed completely in the moment. So, when I got to one particular corner of the room, I could feel the energy was different. I could see a blurred image of a man standing there. He had dark hair and I sensed his loved one would be coming, and he didn't want to be late.

In order for me to sense him, I used intuition and knew I wasn't on autopilot. Since I was in the moment, paying attention to my surroundings, I was able to notice the difference in the energy in that one spot in the room where he stood. I was then able to detect that he was waiting for his loved one to arrive. Later on that night, he showed himself to me again, but this time with balloons. I was tickled to tell his wife that he had arrived before she did and with balloons in hand. She laughed when I told her this because they were going to release balloons on the anniversary of his passing which was the next day. She knew it was him that came early too because he was always punctual and never wanted to be late!

You have the power within yourself to do this as well. It just takes time and practice. The key is to start ruling over your mind instead of it ruling over you. Get the wild toddler in check, and pay more attention to the sweet intuitive underdog in your mind. This will help you understand your intuition and you will gain more trust in yourself. If you implement all the steps and advice I've given so far in this book, I know it can happen for you as it did for me. Tapping into your intuitive side will bring you closer to who you truly are. It will lessen your stress, spiritualize your thinking and doing, and create more peace in your life.

HOMEWORK

- Be in the moment! Every time your thoughts wander to the past or future, come back to the present and place your attention to whatever you are doing.

- Create a "worry box" if your mind is constantly thinking about all sorts of things that only cause you stress and anxiety. Write down the worry and put it in the box. Give your box a name like "GUS" (God, Universe, Spirit) and set the intention that you are handing the problem to Him and letting Him take care of the worry instead.

- Make a to-do list for your daily and/or weekly tasks. This will help you sort some of those crazy thoughts. It gets those thoughts out of your head and on paper so they don't have to keep coming up to remind you about them.

CHAPTER 7
TALKING WITH YOUR ANGELS

Now, the step most of you have been waiting for! Hopefully, you have been able to practice some of the homework given to you in the previous chapters. In order to really take advantage of what you read here, you will have to have practiced some of those exercises.

In truth, everyone is psychic, and I do believe anyone can become a medium. Some are just born more sensitive to angels, the spiritual realm, and their innate gifts than others. This doesn't mean you can't be. It just means that it may require more work on your part, especially if you are more left-brained and logical. Speaking to the spiritual realm requires more imaginative skills. This is why you often see more women in this field, as we tend to be more open to our creative side than men and are naturally more right-brained.

Even though I was exposed to Tarot and other divination tools when I was a teenager, I really didn't know I had a gift until after I went on my spiritual journey, which happened after my seizures started. Up until that point, I was interested in all things psychic, but never had a reading. I watched television shows like *The Long Island Medium* and other programs involving mediums, wondering how they were doing what they were doing. I was incredibly jealous that they had this gift, and I didn't. Why couldn't I have been so lucky to be born a "chosen" one?

Now, I know that no one person is more special than another. We ALL have this gift. We were all born as connectors of the Universe. Think about it. We are sparks of the Divine who manifested into human form. We are the Universe experiencing a very difficult, temporary, but scary time on this planet in an earthly existence. Of course, we would be able to 'phone home' and have support when we came here!

It's like seeing your children off to summer school. They're scared and not sure what to expect, but you would ensure they had everything they needed that you could think of, right? You would be available if they needed you, but you wouldn't smother them. You wouldn't want to take away from their experience at camp. You would simply be available when they needed you. If they had a bad day, they could talk to you. If they needed advice, wouldn't you give them a little bit of help? Well, same goes while we're here visiting Earth.

We are more supported and loved than we could ever imagine. Spirit doesn't just come down here right in front of us to tell us the "truth." It remains a slight mystery for a few reasons. First, our human mind can only comprehend so much. The other reason is, we came here to Earth wanting this amnesia. If we remembered everything from every experience we've ever had through all lifetimes, this whole human experience wouldn't be as much fun. It would lose its "punch." We ALL have angels who act as messengers for us, guides assigned to us to help us on our path. Our loved ones will also support us after they cross over. We all have our phone or antenna to use when we wish to call home, get some insight, and feel a little better.

Here are some of the most common ways they communicate with us. These apply for everyone in the spiritual realm including your angels, spirit guides, and passed loved ones. I call this group your Spiritual Posse.

<u>Thoughts!</u> We already went over this, but I felt I had to put it here again so you wouldn't forget. The most powerful way that angels talk to you is through thought! I had no idea until I started developing my mediumship that this was how it all worked. So, if you're thinking of someone who passed, it isn't always you originating the thought, but them! Have you ever listened to a song and it reminded you of someone who passed? It was likely them making the song come on the radio at that time, placing the thought into your mind. Not the other way around. That is why meditation and mindfulness is key in developing and understanding your intuition. It helps you learn what voice is yours, and what voices are coming from another source.

<u>Numbers!</u> They say the world was built on numbers, and everything is mathematically precise. So, it doesn't surprise me that the spiritual realm is so comfortable using them. You may have heard about angel numbers, but not all of these come from them. Our loved ones who have passed onto the Other Side may also send us numbers as signs. Be on the lookout for numbers like 111, 222,

333, and 444. Or more personal numbers such as your favorite number or your birthdate.

Nature: Angels and loved ones also send signs through nature, such as feathers, birds, butterflies, and the like. It's easy for them to manipulate the energy of these things. We live on a much denser and lower vibrating place than they do, thus it's easier for them to connect to something that is alive. It's easier for them to move that type of energy.

Signs: Another way they speak is through literal signs, messages you might see relayed on billboards, license plates, and bumper stickers. Pay attention to what is brought to your attention while you are driving or riding in a vehicle.

Music: This is such a big sign that Spirit uses to send messages, and most of all, show us we're loved! Take notice of whom or what you are thinking about when you hear a song play that totally catches your attention. If you think of someone, reach out to that person. Or if they're passed, asked for more signs from them. If you stay in the moment, and don't rush the process, I know you'll get more signs to show you WHO exactly is sending you those signs!

Dreams: They may also talk to you in dreams. I often find this as a means to communicate to you so you're not scared when you see them in real life, or to prep you for signs that you might see while you are awake. This applies to passed loved ones too. If you're dreaming of them, and the dreams stop, know they didn't leave you. They are just taking the training wheels off and are waiting for you to notice the signs during the day. That is truly when we need them. During the day hours, we are awake and making choices they could possibly help us with. Nighttime isn't the best time to expect help because we are trying to rest and need to turn off our minds.

Coincidences: Remember, there is no such thing! So, when something happens that seems to be a coincidence, it is truly a mini miracle. If you are thinking of a loved one, and then meet someone with their same name, this could be a sign they are reaching out to you. Perhaps, you are missing someone who passed. You see their birthdate on a license plate. You smile thinking of them and turn on the radio, and the song that is playing was a song they LOVED! This is very likely a sign from them. All of these "coincidences" are not really coincidences; they are signs from Spirit saying they are with you, talking to you, and guiding you!

It is so very important to talk back to your angels and loved ones when you get these signs. Believe in the signs they send you and ask for more. If you are unsure who is sending you the sign, ask them to clarify with another sign. Analyze the sign to see if there's a personal touch to it. For example, when I see the number 83, I know this is from my grandma because she passed when she was 83. Feel free to talk to them and assign them their own numbers so you will know who the sign is from. Also, if you want to know what path to take in life, talk to them and ask them! They really are here to help. All you have to do is be aware that they are sending you those signs. We are often mixed-up in our everyday life. If we're too much in our own mind we won't notice them. If you get one of these signs like we discussed, trust that it is from them. If you are still weary, ask for another sign to confirm. Just be patient with them.

If you have been trying to see these signs and have attempted to receive messages from the Other Side yet can't do it, there could be a couple of things that are keeping the messages from coming in. You may be trying too hard; when you have a thought, you actually send it out to the Universe, and the more you think that thought the more it is multiplied. This is why remaining positive is so crucial-no doubts allowed. Once a thought is multiplied, it comes right back to you! So, if you're thinking and/or saying, "I never get signs. It never *ever* happens!" The Universe responds, saying "Ok, she never gets signs because she keeps saying and thinking it multiple times, so it must be true! The Universe gives you back more of what you tell them. Therefore you receive no signs related to what you really want.

Another possible reason you may not get signs when you ask for them is that you aren't a clear enough vessel-yet. The Other Side operates on a much higher frequency than we humans do. Think about dogs and how they can hear high-pitched sounds that we can't. This is similar to speaking with Spirit. You have to raise your vibration so that you can hear them clearly.

Here are three things that contribute to lowering your vibration that could make it more difficult for you to hear messages:

<u>Lower vibrating emotions</u>. Remember how I said everything is energy? That includes your emotions. Emotions translated means, "Energy in Motion." The higher the vibrational emotion you are feeling, the easier it will be for you to connect. The emotion of joy is one of the highest emotions. If you are following the other steps I've discussed in this book —protecting your energy and grounding—you have already helped to raise your vibration. Just by doing those important steps, your body and mind should feel better and your aura healthier so that you can connect more efficiently. Then, too, if you practice self-care and eat things that align with your body's needs, you will automatically become a higher vibration for Spirit because your body will not be bogged down with

toxins and other bad things. However, if you are suffering from lower vibrational emotions like fear, and depression, it can make it more difficult to hear because you're at too low of a vibrational frequency to hear them.

<u>Highly processed foods</u>. We spoke about this briefly in the Eating Happy chapter, but if you are consuming a lot of processed foods or "dead" products this may not allow the life force energies inside of your body to move very well. These types of foods, therefore, may make it more difficult for you to raise your vibration high enough to hear them.

<u>Drama</u>. When you are involved in things such as gossip, mental abuse and the like, it causes your mind to be wrapped up in the emotions of lower vibrations. It's almost like you are only as good as your lowest emotion. This means that if you experience many emotions at one time, even if one of them is joy, but another is a lot of fear, then your vibrational strength will only be as strong as the fear, which is the lowest vibrating emotion of them all.

The great news is turning this around is easy. Just turn towards doing the opposite of the above. Eat living foods like plants, rather than choosing to ingest a lot of processed products. Refrain from gossip and drama as much as you can, as this will put you well on the way to becoming a clear vessel for Spirit to communicate with you. The more you practice all of these things, the easier it will be for you to see, hear, and feel Spirit.

Just as man has laws, the Universe has laws as well. One of the most bitter-sweet laws we have is free will. This means the spiritual realm cannot intervene in our lives without our permission. We must give them permission to help us. It may seem obvious at times that you want help, but Spirit can't assume that you don't want that opportunity away from you. They see all of life's challenges as possibilities for us to learn and grow. However, they can assist us if we ask them for help. If you're having a hard time in life and you're feeling lost, be sure to talk with your angels or passed loved ones and let them know they are free to intervene. They may not make the situation go away, but could have you stumble across an online article that could help you, or maybe they will create a situation so you will cross paths with someone who could help you.

There is a cute story I heard of once—about how many of us were done with our lives here on Earth and were decided not to reincarnate again. We were retired, but Spirit started recruiting us to come out of retirement and back to Earth because so many humans needed help. The reasoning for this is that humans listen to other humans. Isn't that the truth? We may go against our own instinct and fight our intuition, but we so freely take advice from others. Spirit knows this and will put people in our lives to help us! Be on the lookout for these people whom Spirit has put into your life to help and guide you.

Be aware that your first communication with Spirit may happen as you fall asleep because this is a time when you are trying to calm your mind. For many of us, this may be the first time of the day where you're trying to tame your thoughts (so you can fall asleep). It can also happen shortly upon awakening. This is a perfect time for Spirit to communicate with you because you haven't started up your crazy busy mind yet. If we do more unwinding during the day, we can expect to experience more communication during the day, and less at night. If you don't want to have communication at night time, then just declare your wishes and shield yourself in a bubble of white light.

If you are finding it difficult to communicate with your angels in the ways listed above, I encourage you to use a divination tool. A divination tool allows you to communicate with Spirit using an instrument. Tarot cards, pendulums, crystal balls, and runes are all examples of divination tools. They can help you confirm what you are feeling, what path you feel drawn to, and can really strengthen your bond with spirit. Always ask your angels, loved ones, and guides to bring forth information of 100% pure love and light. We always want to make sure we are gaining insight from the highest vibrational energies from source.

Be sure to write your experiences down. These notes you write will pile up and soon you will realize that it isn't your imagination. You will start to see a transformation take place in your daily living and begin to understand the smaller details that paint the larger picture for you.

It is important to be grateful for any sign you might receive, no matter how big or how small it seems to be. If you come from a place of being thankful, the Universe gives back the appreciation you put out multiplied. For me personally I tell the Universe that I am thankful all of the time and about all the little things. Of course, I thank the Universe every day for my family, friends, and job, but I also thank them for parking spots, good traffic, a cute outfit, and anything good that happens. When I leave for work each morning, it is still dark and I always take a moment to stop and look at the moon. For some reason, the moon just fascinates me. I take a breath, as I stare into the starlit sky and thank the Universe for that moment. It is a great way to start my day. I thank the Universe with my whole heart each and every time. I give all the credit to the Universe, the angels, my guides, and to all of my loved ones who have passed for pretty much everything that happens in my life. This is one of the reasons why

I think I get so many signs and so much support. They know I appreciate them and everything they do. I invite you to give your thanks to the Universe as often as you can as well. As the late Louise Hay said, "The Universe loves grateful people." And I couldn't agree more.

HOMEWORK

- Think about times when you have noticed signs from Spirit. Perhaps you found a feather or a coin. Write these down and who you think the message or sign came from. Then start looking out for these signs, writing them down when they happen. Go back and compare your notes. Are there any patterns? Take note of what is bothering you or what is going on in your life during these times.

- Keep a dream journal if you don't already do so. Write down your dreams as soon as you wake up so that you can remember as much of them as possible. Look back on your notes after a couple of days. You may not be able to determine the dream's significance right away, but reading it at a later time may help you see what your dreams are trying to tell you.

- Watch an episode of one of the psychic medium shows on television, or find a medium presentation on YouTube to view. Notice how they use symbols and signs when they translate any messages from Spirit.

CONCLUSION

My life has changed drastically since I applied these steps into my life. I went from being sick, ridden with anxiety and feeling all alone to a pretty healthy spiritual leader, with a strong bond with my spiritual team. My life isn't perfect, and I know there's more challenges on their way, but I know I don't have to do it alone, and neither do you.

Take advantage of your spiritual posse we talked about and know they are ready to lend a helping hand. Life is tough and can get pretty crappy at times. No matter how big or small your problems are, let them help. I promise you, they don't mind! They are here to help you. Know that even though you may not have a human in this world that can understand you, you have a group of spiritual guys and gals within a mind's reach, ready to support and help you. *Let them*!

FURTHER READING

The Four Agreements by: Miguel Ruiz

Assertiveness for Earth Angels by Doreen Virtue

Don't Sweat the Small Stuff and it's all small Stuff: Simple Ways to Keep the little things from taking over your life (Don't Sweat the Small Stuff Series

Breathe: The Simple, Revolutionary 14-day Program to Improve Your Mental and Physical Health
by: Dr. Belisa Vranich

Can't Hurt Me: Master your Mind and Defy the Odds By: David Goggins

How to Heal Your Body by Louise Hay

I see Dead People: How I learned to Help Earth Bound Spirits by Jane Ross

Soul Contracts: Finding Harmony and Unlock Your Brilliance

How to Hear Your Angels by Doreen Virtue

ABOUT THE AUTHOR

Heather Danielle is a spiritual teacher, psychic medium, and intuitive life coach. She is dedicated to empowering others to embrace their unique gifts so that they can transform their lives beyond their wildest dreams.

She loves drawing cartoons, daydreaming, and playing chess. She is a self-proclaimed free-spirit who never misses an opportunity to talk. She currently resides in the Metro Detroit area with her husband and teenaged son who both talk as much as she does. They spend warm Michigan days riding and practicing tricks on their BMX bikes.

Heather is the author and illustrator of her first book—a children's publication titled *The Day the Sun Slept In*—which is available now at Amazon.com. She is currently working on her third book, which is expected to be published in 2020.

E-mail Heather: heather@riseintoyourpower.com

Visit Website: https://www.riseintoyourpower.com

Printed in Great Britain
by Amazon